12088086

10655459

UBLIN

WALKING ON WATER

JOHN F. DEANE

DUBLIN

Sup.

u09410071

The Dedalus Press
24 The Heath
Cypress Downs
Dublin 6W
Ireland

© 1994 John F. Deane

"Icarus" series number three, 21 April 1994.

UNIVERSITY COLLEGE LIBRARY
19 1994

ISBN 1 873790 53 8 (paper)
ISBN 1 873790 54 6 (bound)

Acknowledgments to: *The Irish Times, The Poetry Ireland Review, PN Review, The Steeple, UNDR*. The poems in the section entitled "Far Country" were published as a limited edition chapbook in 1992.

for Ursula
and for Laura, Catherine and Mary

Cover drawing by John Behan.

Dedalus Books are represented & distributed abroad by Password (Books) Ltd., 23 New Mount St., Manchester M4 4DE

821 IR
DeA

Out on the current a black hag swam,
bright eye, and head erect; again and again it dived
down on its own blackness, exploratory, in hope ...

CONTENTS

IV. *Entering A Picture*

V. *Walking On Water*

VI. *Lives Of The Fathers*

1

The Old Red House

GOING BACK

The train is hurrying west, into the past;
young people, leaning forward,
dream in one another's eyes while an elder,
with thick-lensed spectacles,

head packed tidily inside his cap, builds
whiskey onto whiskey till he grows garrulous;
telegraph poles, like the old people,
lean in out of the wind,

their lines of communication gone;
here is the thistle-crowded peat ocean,
a world of umber, distance, silences –
still in the shadow of the mountain;

how the heart lifts, in recognition!
We stop beside a train on the other tracks;
people gaze towards us and we
watch beyond them, back into ourselves,

wondering, at last, which of us is moving.

REVENANT

Since the last death the old red house
has stood neglected,
the sky has broken through

and winter drips down steadily;
like whispered words out of the past
rusty butterfly wings lie scattered about the floor;

I have come back, a watchful animal
rooting for nourishment;
here I would build a cell to emulate

the head-down obduracy of the fathers
and trust at last to the wilderness within;
but always the crack from a rifle in a field

scatters my gathering revenants; the wings
flutter a moment in the breeze and settle
back in peace when the door closes.

KILLEEN

Children's voices carry from the shore;
a high-tide line of jelly-fish –
sea-spawn, slime – lies waiting;
dangerous waters these, to venture into ...

I stand on a high earth-bank
where winds come probing from the sea;
familiar and unknown worlds
touch in the clay beneath me;

the children – as if all flesh were sin –
lie here, unnamed, their guttural pleadings
carrying from the past;
they, too, were lifted out

from blood-confusion, but were put aside
here on the edge of our world
with sea-smoothed stones lying over them;
the famine road to the ocean's edge

has been tarmacadamed for the caravans;
but our wheels circle these disasters
while the crumbling earth, piecemeal,
reveals the bones of our sad fathers.

THE VALLEY

We left the car, aslant, on cropped grass
and began up the long slope of the valley

hoping, for a while, the heart in its yearning
would be stilled in activity of the climb.

We moved through wet peat-meadows
among curlew, godwit, heron,

and once a snipe
burst from a grass-tuft into dangerous air.

We came down over the ridge to boley villages,
listening for echoes of community, laughter, song,

hoping to put our fingers on the past, for hold :
scatterings of stones, like raided nests,

a crushed-in can among the ferns – nothing more.
The wind was playing organ-music

on the jagged edges of a sheep's skull;
above, the mocking *kraaaa* of a grey crow

disturbed from its feed of skull meat.
This soft-peat world would suck us down to flint bones.

Yet still we are climbing, and still the skald
worries the same sour gristle;

and we will go on climbing, as others climb
over the same, treacherous slopes, yearning.

HALLOWMAS

We raise them up, all saints,
beyond the thresholds of our ignorance
where we can pray to them, and plead;

they are boats
moored to the pettiness of our concerns
and we will not set them free;

we raise them up, all souls,
pumpkins with their brains on fire
where we can pray for them, and fear;

and they come, the dead, blindfolded,
rushing down the tiled hallway,
their hands, out of darkness, reaching for us

who are boats
moored to the pettiness of our concerns;
and the dead won't set us free.

HERITAGE

My parents' people
charted their inward sea of peatland,
pegs hammered down, lines taut between them;

they bent, and dug, and saved, while I
holding the reins, stood on the cart-shafts
legs apart and balancing –

Aeneas setting out, with
yup there yup! to the old ass;
now I explain the process

to my children on the road before me,
drain, bank, scraw, bog-banquet tea;
leave this waste, I tell them,

to lie in peace a thousand years
it will put down roots and, unlike man,
recreate its rich, soft flesh.

A heron stands, still as a shape of bog-oak;
eels have squirmed, like memories, back into the pools.
I turn towards the white-washed villages

and would escape, half-willingly, this wilderness,
shake from my shoulders
my parents' people's weight of faith.

GHOST

I sat where she had sat
in the fireside chair
expecting her to come down the stairs
into the kitchen;

the door was open, welcoming;
coals shifted in the Rayburn,
a kettle hummed;
she heard the sussurrations of the fridge,

she had surrounded herself with photographs,
old calendars, hand-coloured picture-postcards;
sometimes a robin looked in at her from the world
or a dog barked vacantly from the hill;

widowed she sat, in the fireside chair,
leaning into a populated past;
she sat so quietly, expecting ghosts,
that a grey mouse moved by, uncurious

till she stomped her foot against the floor;
and did she sense, I wondered, the ghost
who would come after her death to sit
where she had sat, in the fireside chair?

THE OLD RED HOUSE

I stand head-high over the attic beams
among bones of roof and window-frame,
the new house waiting for its covering of flesh;

starling, swallow, swift
fly urgently as wishes
through the wind-filled spaces;

the blocks are rough, uneducated yet
to the principles of our living, but soon
I will be hoarding into dark places

the books and cutleries, the heirlooms,
for we have raided the stores of the old, red house
against the day the roof will tumble in,

exposing dried-out marrow of the rafters,
the wizened felt, like skin,
the skeletal frames of starling, swallow, swift.

II

POSTULANT

"Come with a thought, I thank thee, spirit, come!"

POSTULANT

✢

We turned in off the main road
between high pillars and undisturbed
aristocratic trees, the fug of silence

thickening between us
after the slow voyage across Ireland;
there was a long meandering driveway

through meadowlands towards an island of trees,
terror rising in me as the car rounded
on a gravel foreshore, where others

stood at the shuddering end of boyhood,
presented, and received, at the Lord's door.
Granny, corsetted from the last century,

held me awhile, in silence, at a loss,
taut with pride and loneliness;
pray for me, she whispered, but I am come

to gather myself together, to become all Ariel.
(Pray for us, the rearguard generation,
aground, washed up by the last high tide.)

I watched the small red tail lights
of the old Ford Prefect
negotiate the driveway back into the sixties.

✢

He came in through the top door –
moody, mantled, Lord of our strange isle –
and stood behind the table, watching us;
at once a shiver of guilt ran in my blood;

he sat; we sat; and he began :
the company of men ...
Of fixed purpose, wing-dip, swoop,
he was a harrier, pitched high

and haughty, with some disdain
testing and troubling us,
urging us, starlings, one from the other
into our own untrusted loneliness;

*each time I go out among mankind
I return a lesser man ...*

✢

The seminary, still as a village before the dawn.
Hunched figures come, rummaging through our dreams.
When the bell has called for the third time

we will unhook huge shadows from the door and tie them on.

We shift and sigh in choir like an avenue of trees.
When the world stirs we will be still again,
shivering and solitary on exposed headlands.

12088086.

✣

Exercise, he told us,
the small, stiff muscle of holiness;
and day after day we came

in threes, through the cloister door,
taking our places,
black figures, pacing

the cinder track around a field,
hurrying in the chase,
wisdom always disappearing

ahead of us, and our God,
from his high vantage-point,
cheering us on.

✛

After the soft *noctem* of the Latin chant
we faced, till dawn, into a Great Silence;
we were a flock of isolated starlings
settling in the rich foliage of an oak;

all day a small brass crucifix lay heavily
on the pillow; I held and kissed it, then
folding my hands across my breast,
lay down again into medieval darkness.

+

I was beckoned in to the harness shed;
the brother stood, red-faced, jocular and poised,
a sheep held fast between his knees,

the grey-white wool matted and soiled,
the eyes far-seeing. I held her, gently,
but she slipped and dragged from me,

hooves skittering across the cobblestones;
a humane killer, drill-perfect, primed,
was touched to the skull, the trigger touched;

I imagined the bullet eating
like a bit through bone. The suddenness
took me, the instantly yielded weight

and we fell together at the brother's feet;
I was sent back to flower-beds and grass verges;
come! book one, chapter one, in the beginning God ...

III

Far Country

i.m. Daniel Patrick Deane (1908 – 1991)

ON ANOTHER SHORE

The worn-out Otherthing
rigid on its slab, the fluids
stagnant;
dressed up and parcelled – the Offence;

someone had set a plastic rose
upon the chest,
and we, attendants,
faces unmasked by grief,

murmured our studied words :
he is not dead, but sleeping,
he is not here,
he has stepped out on another shore

beautiful beyond belief;
and we have crept back out
into weakened sunshine,
knowing our possibilities

diminished.

THE CURRENT

He stood, up to his thighs in slip-water,
spinning; concentrated, eager, his hands
exact with rod and water-coloured gut;

I was digging in sand behind him, safe
from the wildering rush of the current;
periwinkles breathed small bubbles in the pools

and barnacles clung to the rough rock surfaces;
I hammered on their backs with stones
and watched the water-blood

seep from the shattered shells;
sometimes the shoals of mackerel broke
into the shallows near him, famished,

frenzied through the living mercury of eels;
I pictured them, out there, the shoals,
streaming through the cold, inhuman forests

of the underworld, aghast, and wraithlike.
When he made his way homeward over rocks
mackerel were strung by their gills on twine,

fish-scales, fish-blood, ghosting his clothes
and I beside him, quietened,
clinging to his rough, red hands, for hold.

FERRY

The waves between the islands
were dark green walls
rising against us;

I cried with the thrill of it,
the throbbing vessel hoisted high and held –
while we watched a moment

towards our fall, that
helplessness, down down down;
his face was bright with merriment, his glasses

wet from sea-spray; there were sea-birds
– auk and guillemot and shearwater –
in their element, about us;

too soon we reached harbour, the boat
juddering clouds of silt through the water,
thud of wooden taffrail against concrete;

I grew nervous then for his big body
stepping out between gunwale and pier,
my small hand stretched up uselessly to help;

shorefall, the pale road upwards,
distances, and waves between the islands
rising again between us.

WHEEL

Northwards the rain
brushed grey over the world; westwards
distance, black impasto clouds;
in a blunt Ford Prefect

smelling of oil, tobacco,
I held the big, moulded, driving wheel;
around us the obstacles
were sheep, and hare-track culverts,

and there – the future, beyond the dashboard,
out over the bonnet, a huge
and virgin canvas. Father,
straight-backed and tender,

held my fingers on the wheel;
noon, and stillness, the first day.
And still he is gazing
out the rear window

over sand-dunes, strand and waves,
the skin of his face
finger-applied out of limed clay;
God's image,

in waistcoat and shirt,
the small stud dangling. Still
life. While far away, in the background
a milk-white gannet dives into the sea.

SCYTHE

He has been moving
on the widening circumference
of a circle of his own making;

eye bright, back straight, and head erect;
his shirt-sleeves folded, sweat on his flesh,
intoxicating clover-pollen

rising to him, and the high grass –
in breathless ballet – falling at his feet;
he has achieved a rhythm

that takes him from us for a while,
his soul a hub of quietness,
his body melting into the almost perfect

elliptical orbitting of the world;
soon he will flop down tiredly amongst us,
his thoughts, as after sex, turning

on the heroes of myth and literature
while the grass at the centre of his circle
has begun, imperceptibly, to green.

ISLANDMAN

1.

As in a book of origins
he comes striding down a long valley,
cartridge-belts ebullient across his chest,
the rifle riding gently on his arm;
mountains lift their names about him –
Bunowna, Croghaun, Bunnafreva, Keem;

clouds rip themselves against high craglands;
I, cowering in his potency,
hear the distant pounding of the ocean,
the sky is filled with all the space
between Achill and America;
up in the hills, the mountain goats run free;

the peat floor is treacherous,
eager, like time, to take its prey
and hold it in its juices; he has climbed
slopes salted with gull-droppings,
paused by the old stone boleys;
I whisper my name into the bowl of time –

his head jerks upwards, and he frowns.

2.

The long hay-loft was low
and raftered like the island chapel;
among the undersides of slates,
snow-falls of plaster, star-holes,
he taught me how to climb from beam to beam,
my feet never touching the ground;

he showed me how to fall, cat-soft,
into mothering hay, and I never dreamed
the rough stone floor of the future;
once I dressed up to look like him,
strutting with waders, cartridge-belts and rifle;
now he is in my words, my diffidence,

he has been dressing himself again in my flesh.

3.

Island. Still point
in a turbulent sea. A man, among others,
islanded, pacing the shore
or stalking winter geese through a chill dusk;
old Sarah Coyne, sidling and grinning,
comes showing her withered arm

and there! cracked Willie Slate
pissing on the road before the tourists –
anything, to keep the prowler from the heart;
war reports on the wireless, and de Valera
pelted with stones at Achill Sound.
It is easy to say "I love you" to the dead,

the words are a hard, packed ball
beaten and beaten against a high, blank wall;
but he whispers his name to me still,
comes striding down a long valley,
mountains lifting their names about him –
Bunowna, Croghaun, Bunnafreva, Keem.

FUGITIVE

Old man, in corded, ripe-plum dressing-gown,
sitting out, and silent; beyond high windows
are blood-bright tulips, funerary
wind-blown daffodils. Love comes

blundering about him; he
holds himself apart, intent upon his going,
abandons me mid-sentence, my words
all, like petals, falling about my feet.

THE CIRCLE

1

Darkness. Wind about the house brushing against our walls. I could sense, through shut eyelids, the lighter shade of curtains between the blacknesses within and those without.

In the new suburbs there are no trees to soften the winds and to give them names. We huddle among painted bricks and rafters, alarms primed to scream, hoping the foliage will grow, quickly, round us.

I folded my body up under the electric blanket. The wind, not animal, tore clematis from the garden walls, knocked down the sweet, red-painted, bird-tables. After a time, I slept.

2

Old man naked. Laid on a farmhouse kitchen table, on thick, scrubbed timbers. His long body the colour of sour cream. His hands along the timbers, raw, at his sides. The chest-hair thick, grey-white. The face, inscrutable, as always. Vague figures shifting round him, presences, unnamed. I see the wild and wintering grey-lag, shot.

Again. I stand above. Below, a patch of earth. Black clay. Cleared ground. Huddled at a distance, in heavy coats, halt, people. Indistinct, but shocked. Old man naked. The body whiter than known white. Lying at the edge of the earth, at an angle. Knees drawn up, birthing, hands raised above the head, pleading innocence. I see the wild and wintering grey-lag, shot. Soon, I wake.

3

He was sitting at the foot of a bed, on a high, hospital chair. I noticed the steel end of the bed, the steel handle, like the cranking-handle of an old Ford Prefect. The sheets rigid with white, the counterpane, light-blue, smoothed out. He was sitting perfectly still, hands on his lap, head lowered. The pink, bare skull, the few white hairs on the nape of the neck. The collar of his dressing-gown had one side folded in on itself. Small tufts of hair in his ear.

Old man. Exposed to the wildering rush of the current.

He was turned at an angle from me, motionless. And knowing. He had taken himself already a great distance from the ward. I was reluctant to bring him back. Through the wide, hospital window, the rough sea-shore of rooftops. I touched him on the shoulder. He turned his face towards me, gathering himself back out of his preparations. And looked. My own, tense face, staring, unseeing, up at me. Frightened. Tear-full. The hands, reaching upwards, for hold.

FAR COUNTRY

1.

He told us Pushkin, Tolstoy, Gogol;
we were Tatar and Cossack, I was Taras Bulba

leading moustachioed hordes over drain and árdán,
my short pants wide as the Black Sea,

Bunnacurry the Ukraine
and Stony River the Dnieper.

2.

I watched him
pacing the stone flags of the kitchen floor,
hands in his pockets, eyes cast down;

but he was ranging across the steppes of his imagination,
bright meadow, ballroom, serf,
the immensity of his white land, his far country.

3.

For years he worked at a deal table
cumbered with files and documents
while a harassed people, rough-handed, old,
came to him with forms;

sometimes he held a match to a stub of wax
and watched its one big drop of blood
fall heavily. His eyes were glazed with dust,
his long legs, under the table, curled.

4.

Together we stepped down onto the tarmac,
he was silent, pleading,

home at last, reach, toe-tip, hold
like Daedalus after his hazardous flight;

old now, and slow, he was entering through the sliding
glass doors of his dream,

suffering the long
low customs hall, passport control,

questioned for currency, for proof
he was who he thought he was and no other.

5.

By day we were Intourists, on an Intourist bus,
viewing mechanical glories of the Revolution.
We queued for hours to see the saint,
shambling, like convicts, between rows of guards;

stepped down, out of the sun, into a crypt,
where Lenin lies, uncorrupted, under glass,
plans for the reconstruction of the world
frozen in his head; a dead man's bedroom

but you cannot touch the folded hands
or put your lips to the alabaster brow.
Father was silent, pleading; at night I heard him
turn in his bed, utter small, hurt, animal cries.

6.

At last, at dawn, in the airport terminal,
I saw him sitting, radiant

under the chandeliers of Russian words,
speaking with an old official at a desk

who dropped wax blood onto yellow forms;
they spoke of weather, traffic, snow,

of Pushkin, Tolstoy, Gogol,
the summer and winter palaces

that were still standing
bright as birthday cakes in their fair country.

ON THIS SHORE

They laid him on his back
in the flat-bottomed
ramshackle boat that the dead use
and carried him down to the shore;

quickly he sank
into the current's hold
and did not come up again for air;
when I had kissed his forehead

he was already cold
and had begun to sweat;
soon he will have shed all baggage,
the great gannet of life

will be gliding over him like a dream;
he has cast off at last
from the high white cross
to which he was anchored

and I have turned back,
carrying his burden,
leaving a deeper set of footprints
across the sand.

IV

Entering a Picture

i.m. Mary Jo Connors (1908 – 1986)

SCHOOL

I was sent in with messages,
the school a cottage
crockery-bright with learning;

chalk-dust made rhymes
along shafts of sunlight,
her words pitched high,

her angers disconcerting
as the squeals of chalk-stubbs
against the blackboard;

the girls were in ranks before her,
their hair, their smell, the giggling
while I, in my short pants,

walked the no-man's land towards her;
as I come now, still
hesitant, offering

lines of sorrow
towards the understanding
she has taken with her into silence.

MIRROR

I was young enough
to be allowed to rummage in the big room
while she prepared herself for the day;
I could stand in the window recess,
draw the curtains and be invisible;

unguents and oils on the dressing-table,
combs and brushes, talc – such mysteries;
sometimes her face was a ghost's face
smeared with cream; now I believe
she sat before the big, hinged mirror

watching through the window towards another life
where she waltzed at the sea's edge,
where the moon was an orange over palm trees;
I saw her turn back towards the glass
to wipe the moisture from about her eyes.

WINTER SILENCE

Ice came, regularly as the grey lag,
to lay its weight over the island;
I watched her

pick her way through morning,
step like a high-stilted bird
astonished across its frozen lake;

all afternoon we watched
through reflected images of ourselves
the disconcerting coming down of snow;

sometimes our faces swayed like ghosts
looking in at us from another world;
we wrote out names on glass with our fingertips.

She sat, finally, on the edge of the bed,
her feet dangling;
where are you now? I whispered

searching her face for traces of the dream;
her eyes were glazed, her lips pursed.
Field and hedgerow, after long snowfall,

are like a sheet drawn up
on the newly dead;
we lit tall candles about her cot

and I called again into winter silence :
are you? expecting no reply.
   Came the slow slushing of tyres over a bridge,

procession of cars along a road
that turned with the turns of a river, long
black ribbons binding the earth together;

words bounced back at us from a grey sky
where we stood, drawn close together,
black ghosts adrift through a white world.
Morning

and the world outside was a white ocean
while here, at the ocean's edge,
her name outlined in froth across our pane.

ALBUM

It begins on rocks, the sea
touching the jagged edges gently;
she sits, abstracted, a 1930's beauty
on her like a dream;
only the photographer's shadow falls
slanting towards her flesh;

we come, pilgrims, touching the world awhile,
leave memories, resentments, photographs :
the black and white of youth,
the watersports, fashions, winter slopes,
the certainties
not yet degenerated into hope;

there would have been a ship, and movement,
sophisticated dream-days cruising;
here, she is sitting at a table –
a café near Pompeii;
she is young, immortal, virginal,
lifting her glass, elated, towards the future;

in the album she tried to hold time down,
adding meticulous annotations
in her flowing, teacher's, hand;
until, juddering towards the final port,
she had forgotten the point of her pilgrimage,
and taken to slippers, dressing-gown and chair.

ISLANDS

My God was in the froth the sea created,
words lifted and spun into cloths of air
by the unpredictable winds;

our days by the sea's edge
are but a shadow without stay
while inarticulate angels pass with messages;

around us the ocean of words,
if only you could fling a net
and draw them to you in their thousands!

I found little out of our years to cherish;
she had remained outside the secret shed
of my imaginings, a voice

calling me in for prayers;
what I remember is an old woman,
an old woman's settled ways,

words falling from her treasury like ash;
she chewed her lip over crossword puzzles,
words like *love* and *truth* and *innocence*;

you could envy, I heard her say
in one of her lucid moments, the trees
shedding their vulnerable parts

before the onslaught of sorrow.
After her death I slept, expecting presences,
in the big room where she had slept;

there were only the small items of a life
where she, too, had been labouring towards truth,
the brushes, lotions, rosaries,

my own, strained image in her mirror;
I try to say "I love you" to the dead,
knowing that in the long war I have been slow

to understand we were on the same side.
If only you could start out again,
the island virginal in its shift of snow,

but she has left us long ago to walk
away over the water without a guide;
leaving me words, sorrows, the unpredictable winds.

PEACE

I come – offering my bouquet of sorrow –
to this city outside a city

where everything of life
has turned to rumour;

autumn-coloured cats
lick their claws on the doorsteps and doze

under the citron-yellow disk of the sun;
it is like walking in an elegant century

or entering a picture, stylized, *nature morte* ;
people stoop, in silence, tending memories

while a magpie struts and scolds
on the arms of a high, white, calvary –

God the hub and we the humming,
the restless living here to sue for peace.

LOVE

Like starting on a pilgrimage,
stepping blithely out over the gunwale
hoping to waltz on water;

hands working inside one another's lives,
grasping the heart, for hold.
I heard their voices through the wall

like summer murmuring;
he brought her honeycombs
in wooden frames soft as the host,

a small, hard, ball of wax
stayed forever in her mouth
after the sweetness.

But in the photograph they are still
striding out together along the beach,
smiling, confident,

striding into the confusion
of their final months, their love
a bonding, dulled, unspoken,

they will disappear, exemplary, together
as if the sea had swallowed them,
leave echoes of a low, ongoing, music.

V

Walking on Water

WALKING ON WATER

Again I have been surprised,
returned, suddenly,
to the earth's familiarity;

it is like opening an unfamiliar door
and being welcomed
by the chattering of friends;

I have been walking round among the dead,
reasoning with them, and pleading,
talked of old beliefs, and solid ground,

the ease of breathing in unconfined spaces;
as if I could step out onto the sea
and walk beside them on our journey

into innocence;
while in the cemetery their headstones lean
drowning in the seas of columbine.

* * *

Sometimes through the darkness
the fabulous light from Clare Island
swept like a dancer across the bay;

I slept in its security,
as on other nights, father driving home,
I dozed in the murmuring of voices;

sometimes, like doubt, the sea-mists came
thick and slow-moving
to draw a curtain down across the light,

headlands
appearing and disappearing,
their names that had been memorized like prayers

losing relevance,
when all you had to hold to was
weather-patience, that slow, deliberate plodding of cattle

and everyone about you
moved as ghosts
distraught across their purgatory.

✳ ✳ ✳

Time sits, bemused, on benches
under the stained windows of the chapel
and echoes in the muttering

of the old men's voices : what
does a man gain – they are saying –
for all the stress that he has suffered

under the rain? they say :
the emigrant bus is forever full,
the sea-weed swathes laid out on rocks to dry

are ribs of the dinosaur
and the old, grey-tweed cap will serve
to ease the knee-bone when it comes to prayer.

* * *

I am standing, half-way down the staircase
listening through the banisters to voices
from the living room;

they are playing poker round the table,
there are coins and glasses,
the breathstopping gamble of a shilling;

I am imagining
what it is to be an adult,
the great world at your fingertips :

night gatherings, someone
lifting a glass up against the light,
the stars holding forever their liquid orbit;

and then I turn again, near sleep,
following a candle
upstairs towards the future.

* * *

The winds come driving the salt spray
like herds of cattle over our fields,
crossing from the beginning of time until now;

or they are angels
passing with messages for the midlands
from the unkempt Atlantic :

to you, o God, ten thousand years
are as yesterday,
you come sweeping men away like dreams.

* * *

A perfect moon high above the cliff-mass,
a gravel pathway out over the sea;
a curlew calling from the soul of night;

all the while there was something drifting in
lazily, appearing, disappearing,
like a memory you cannot put a name to;

then, while I slept, the world grew
to storms and driven rain
troubling me, too, in the depths of sleep.

Morning, I walked along the shore;
the body of a great seal lay
thrown up on rocks by the last wave;

it will lie, flippers a baby's fingers in the air,
the sweet, unearthly stench of its going
will ghost its way towards the inland fields.

* * *

Some day man, also, will melt back down to daub;
in the deserted houses of the village
stones jostle each other back into the hill;

up in the abandoned quarry the machines –
tyrannosaur, iguanodon –
are rusting down into their heather beds;

the dumped cars sink in the juices
of the black stomach of the bogs;
some day man, also, will melt back down to daub.

***

On the high slope behind the beach
with each withdrawing wave
a million million almost rounded stones

rush with a hoarse and frantic cheering
that now, at last, is their release :
and are rolled back in on the next wave;

not for a single moment
has there been, nor ever will there be,
silence amongst us, and peace, and rest.

***

Perhaps God is not the shore
on which, like grounded boats, we end
our journeying;

perhaps God
is the ocean we step out on
through death, into our origins.

***

The sea surrounds us in the way, we hope,
God's care surrounds us;
out there, shark bodies

are long and lissom as a whip;
there is brill, black sole and the breadcrumb flesh of crabs
tasting of the essence of sea;

here ravens are riding the air above us, groaning;
and somewhere, circling offshore
there is a seal in mourning, its great love lost;

save me, O Lord, when the waters take my soul.

VI

Lives of the Fathers

THE FATHERS

Packed like sea-birds on a cliff ledge, they soared
out at times in ecstacy through chill air,
and back, scrabbling for hold;
they were loud and rounded, blunt-headed, their

God was a male and blundering Atlantic;
the fathers, lean, hooped in certainty about
themselves, husbanded the mind's light and sucked
on the bones of fabulous, fresh-water trout;

tongues curling, they pinned their God in stylized
butterfly colours onto a parchment page.
Now I – where shall I worship? out of the sun

in baptistries of garages? along aisles
of superstores? with the heart steeled as if the grave
glide to disappointment had not yet begun.

THE WORD

It would seem that this is my condition :
Saturday, between dread and expectation;

starlings have been gathering on the wires
working their coy and wheedling side-steps

while I have been making a Z of my body,
move words about, processing them,

focussing towards the one word : *Christ.*
Pregnant with themselves all year the irises

have flexed their coloured wings upon the air;
I touch my finger to pear-blossom stamens

and see! my finger tipped with life-mercury;
joy in the words, and the words are God.

COMMUNION

for Mary Ursula

This tar-black *tabula rasa,* our before and after;
the endless blue-black blank of space;
here, now, may-blossom, apple-blossom, she –

child in white dress, white veil, a dazzle
under the high lit vault of the Church;
star-music, metallic jangling of keys, motion

like eddies of whirled cream, that long, slow
inward collapse of worlds into being,
snowfall of starflakes forever across space;

if you never dip twice in the same stream
where, then, have you been since the last May?
journeying, pain, some ecstacy, circling back

for the may-fly dance, white irises,
the child in white dress, white veil, a dazzle
startling suburban side-streets for a while;

you never gaze twice on the same star-swirl,
slow-waltzing solitaries, solids, heat at the core;
the small girl, white hands joined, expectant,

mouth open, milk-teeth, tongue, to absorb the God;
may-blossom beauty taking the breath away;
she, too, is crying out of the wilderness,

listening for signals, the stuttering messages of morse;
soon the trees will lean heavily towards fruiting,
and a star, centuries away, will puff! and go out.

THE COMPANY OF MEN

This morning, Sunday,
outside the season of pilgrimage,
I have walked the sea-coast road
disdaining human company,
the honeyed, insinuating voices;

blackberries were stars shining in a green sky
and rose-hips festive bulbs;
the holy mountain rose above me,
firm in its place,
head in the clouds as usual;

the small blue rowing-boat of my faith
has been drawn up beyond the tide-line
and wild flowers of the middle earth
have grown steadily through its timbers;
traffic on the road becomes

rumour of another life; and then
– as if the mud-flats spawned mud-birds –
a heron couple lifted, flapped across the bay,
then landed with a hoarse, challenging scream;
they stood, like fence-posts opposite, insisting :

thus far you come, no further.

READING MARTIN LUTHER IN
COLOGNE CATHEDRAL

There is a rock-band
hammering on metal
across the cathedral square;

I lean back, look up,
the blackened high spires
are pine-tops stilled after birds have flown;

over the Rhine the railway bridge
shudders with trains from the ports and plains of Europe
and far below the huge barge *Kommerz*

works assiduously.
I step inside to the darkness of faith;
under the gothic reach of pillars

kings and queens and cardinals
preside from stone sarcophagi;
here are treasures of another age,

monstrances, reliquaries,
sighs of prayer are antique gold
and bones of virgins clustering dried-up shells.

I close my eyes, like Abraham, but find no voice
calling to me from the wilderness;
tourists in the high Köln Dom

we bob and twitter, finches
pausing for a moment on the high tips of pines
before flying into light.

for Pádraig J. Daly

THE LAKE

A boat, fresh water, father at the oars;
we were hushed in among tall reeds
with mallard, sedge-birds, secrets;

father prepared the lures while around us
the water finger-tapped against our hull;
becalmed; held; on a kindly palm. Drifting.

Before knowledge of depths or silt, of shoals
streaming frenziedly beneath us,
before storms, or the scanning of horizons

for news of a strong, a rescuing presence.

THE WESTPORT TO ACHILL LINE

We in the West had our prophet, too,
our big, red-bearded, ham-fisted man,

boasting the burden of Niniveh, God's wrath
in the iron rattling of flanged wheels;

and the first train a funeral train, do you remember?
and the last! so they closed the railway

that the fathers' sins be not visited on the children.
How they stood, engine and tender, in the station!

steaming with certainties; how they shook the little fields
with the importance of fancied distances!

I followed the line of their old lives
on a high embankment between road and sea

covered with thistles, grass and mould;
I heard the hiss of steam, the high proud whistle

and out from a wood came the slow, ghost train,
faces staring from the carriage windows;

I knew them – father! mother!
I waved but their eyes

were fixed on another destination, the vanished line
curving away to the black mouth of a tunnel;

I put my ear to the hard, packed earth, and heard
nothing; in the abandoned station I stood, waving,

"good-bye!" I called, "good-bye! And please,
at last, and for ever now, good-bye!"

THE MOUNTAIN

It was everywhere, its pyramid
shimmering in light across the bay
or glowering, invisible, behind persistent rains.

Pointing to heaven. Weighing down
lives of the fathers who seem –
in the eyes of the foolish – to have died.

We trudged for hours to master it, a people
gathering in the low drone of language,
trailing into silence as we climbed

laboriously, towards the clouds.
The heavenly hosts, we believed,
were everywhere about us, and we,

appointed something less than angels,
reached eagerly beyond our mortal state –
Christ above me, Christ within ... We rose

till suddenly all the kingdoms of the world –
the panoply of islands,
spells cast by flesh, and smiths, and Druids –

were offered in their wonder far below.
We prayed, circling the loveless summit,
hawks hovering on the shadows of ourselves

a mile high in the chilling, barren air.
Most difficult of all has been the coming
off the mountain, finding hold

on shifting shale and scree,
the slow climb down into the body.
Once back on earth, the boy –

who dreamt among the hillside heathers
a voice had called to him from another world –
saw the mountain fade to the rich truth of myth.